Written by Melisa Neal
LotussAdventures@gmail.com

Edited by Michelle Houts

Designed by Sam Douglas
SamDouglasArt.com

Oh boy! Oh boy! I am watching my human family, and they are getting things together and packed in the truck! We must be getting ready to go on a trip. I just love trips!

I watch closely, because I just know that I might get to go.

Suddenly, Melisa says, "Let's go, Lotus."
Yes, Lotus is my name, and I am one smart girl, I think.

I jump up and run to the door where Melisa and Michael are waiting for me. Melisa opens the door, and we all walk outside and get in the truck. Off we go!

Wow!
These roads wind up and down and around the mountains.
I can't wait to get where we are going and get outside!

Finally, we arrive at the campground where there are lots of trees and grass and even hiking trails. "Ok now, let's all get some rest," Melisa says.

I settle, but I am not able to sleep. I am lying awake and wondering what tomorrow will bring.

The sun comes up as I start to wake up. I wait patiently again with my paws crossed, my chin resting on them, just waiting to see, and...

Yes!

"Let's go on an adventure, Lotus," Melisa says. Melisa, Michael, their friend Elfie and I all load up in the truck and make our way to the top of the mountain.

We stop and I know it. We are going on a hike in the woods! I have a blast hiking down the trail. My tail wags, and I sniff everything. The smells! Oh, the smells! I even smell squirrel tracks.

Our hike is now ending, so we head back to the truck. I know where the truck is because I am a smart girl.

The big bright sun is starting to disappear behind the mountain for the day, and it is getting dark outside.

Suddenly, I smell something—something that I have never smelt before. Sniff, sniff! And right before my eyes—so close—jumps a big white-tailed deer! It puts its head in the air and takes off running, lightning fast.

I take off right behind, running faster and faster. My leash is getting tight. Melisa holds on and tries to keep up, but her arm is stretched out far, and she cannot hold on any longer.
She lets go.

I keep running and jump over a ditch, chasing after the deer. It is fast, and off in the woods it goes. The deer disappears.

Melisa yells my name, and I turn to go back, but my leash is caught on a tree. Oh no! I know she will worry if I do not get back to her. I try to get free, but I cannot.

The sun is now behind the mountain, and it is dark. I start digging and digging to get away. I pull, but I cannot get free, and I am getting tired.

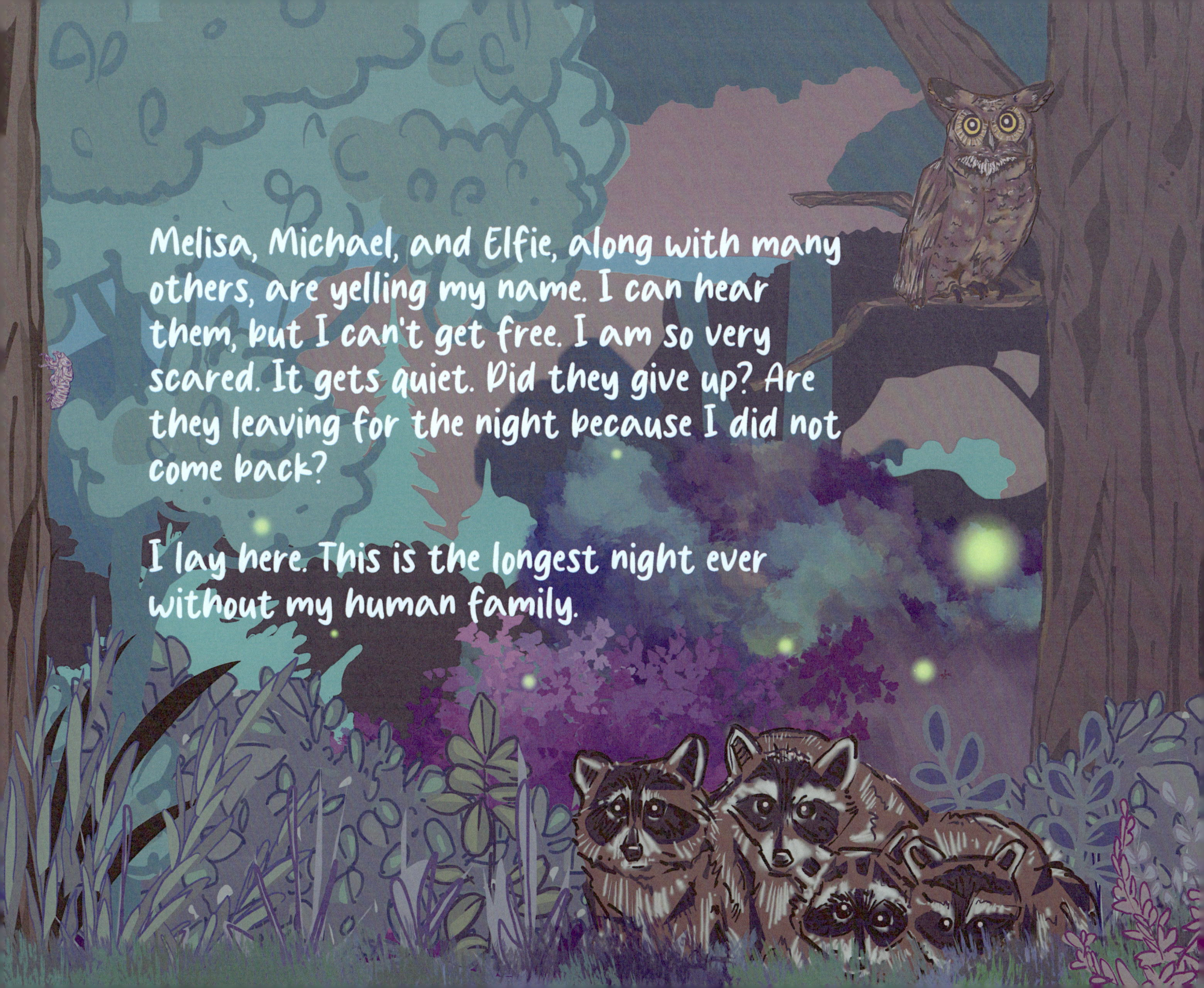

Melisa, Michael, and Elfie, along with many others, are yelling my name. I can hear them, but I can't get free. I am so very scared. It gets quiet. Did they give up? Are they leaving for the night because I did not come back?

I lay here. This is the longest night ever without my human family.

The sun is popping up from behind the mountain. I wake up and try to get away by digging and digging some more.

I wiggle and the snap on my leash suddenly comes undone. I am free! Woohoo!

I can hear lots of voices yelling my name. They started searching again! I run and run to find my way back.

I make it to the road and look over where the truck is parked, remembering I'm smart, and I know where we started out the day before.

When I get back to the truck, the doors are shut. I paw on the door, hoping it will open, but it does not.

I jump in and lay down. I am in a safe spot now. Elfie looks in the window and our eyes meet. She says, "Lotus, you are found and you are ok." She calls Melisa and Michael to tell them the good news. Everyone is so excited.

Melisa, with tears of joy, hugs me tight and gives me some water. I am so thirsty! She looks down and notices my paws. They are so sore, sore from digging and trying to get free. Thank God that I am found and back with my family.

"Let's meet all the people who were searching for you," Melisa says. They are all so nice. They pet me.

Dear Lotus,

I love you so much! You are amazing and I am so thankful to be on this life journey with you. On this day we were both surprised when the deer jumped up right in front of us. Your instincts kicked in and the chase was on. I just could not keep up. When you got out of sight, I got so worried. It was a rollercoaster of emotions that day on this adventure. One minute we were frolicking through the woods, feeling on top of the mountain, and the next in the valley low, separated, then finally reuniting with tears of joy! We both faced, overcame, and learned from our challenges in life. You are such a smart, loving, strong, resilient, happy canine partner that has truly made me who I am today! I am so thankful and grateful for those in our lives who have supported us along the way-our friends, family, and especially Dr. Nita and Dr. Jan for their efforts and caring, loving concern for our best interests and our well-being! A big thank you to Elfie, friends, and her community for their heroic efforts in the search. All were tired, it was a very hot day and long night. Everyone searched miles and miles of the mountainside for you. And I just still wonder how you got free. Your longline was found wrapped around a tree where you had dug at the ground to get free and the snap on your line was not broken. Truly a miracle! Hugs, kisses, and lots of treaties for my girl! Lotus, You're my world!

Love, Melisa

www.ingramcontent.com/pod-product-compliance
Ingram Content Group UK Ltd.
Pitfield, Milton Keynes, MK11 3LW, UK
UKRC050315240426
12049UKWH00019B/172